The Apocryphon of John
(The Secret Book of John)

Mystical Revelations of Creation and Divine Knowledge

A Modern Translation

Adapted for the Contemporary Reader

**John the Apostle
(Gnostic Tradition)**

Translated by Tim Zengerink

Table Of Contents

Preface - Message to the Reader

What If You Could Help Rebuild the Greatest Library in Human History?

Thousands of years ago, the Library of Alexandria stood as the crown jewel of human achievement — a sanctuary where the collected wisdom of every known civilization was gathered, preserved, and shared freely.

And then, it was lost.

Through fire, conquest, and the slow erosion of time, humanity lost not just books — but ideas, dreams, discoveries, and stories that could have changed the world forever.

Today, the Library of Alexandria lives again — and you are invited to be a part of its restoration.

Our mission is simple yet profound:

To rebuild the greatest library the world has ever known, and to translate all timeless works into every language and dialect, so that no seeker of knowledge is ever left behind again.

By joining our movement to rebuild the modern Library of Alexandria, you become part of an unprecedented mission:

- **Unlimited Access to the Greatest Audiobooks & eBooks Ever Written:**

  Instantly explore thousands of legendary works—Plato, Shakespeare, Jane Austen, Leo Tolstoy, and countless more. All instantly available to read or listen, placing a complete literary universe at your fingertips.

- **Beautiful Paperback & Deluxe Editions at Printing Cost**

  Own any title as an elegant paperback, deluxe hardcover, or stunning collectible boxset—offered to you at true printing cost, delivered straight to your door. Build your personal Library of Alexandria, crafted for beauty, built for durability, and worthy of proud display.

- **Fresh Translations for Modern Readers—in Every Language & Dialect**

  Enjoy timeless masterpieces reimagined in clear, contemporary language—no more outdated phrases or obscure references. Alongside the original versions, we're tirelessly translating these classics into every language and dialect imaginable, ensuring accessibility and understanding across cultures and generations.

- **Join a Global Renaissance of Literature & Knowledge**

  You directly support expanding our library, publishing deluxe editions at true cost, translating works into all global languages, and bringing humanity's greatest stories to people everywhere. By joining today, you're not just preserving a legacy of masterpieces; you set in motion a powerful wave of literary accessibility.

Become a Torchbearer of Knowledge.

Join us for free now at **LibraryofAlexandria.com**

Together, we will ensure that the light of human wisdom never fades again.

With gratitude and a shared love of knowledge,

The Modern Library of Alexandria Team

Visit:

www.libraryofalexandria.com

Or scan the code below:

Introduction

The Hidden Revelation and
the Divine Origin of All

The Apocryphon of John, also known as The Secret Book of John, stands as one of the most foundational and revered texts of the Gnostic tradition. Attributed to John the Apostle and written in the second century CE, this revelatory work presents an extraordinary mystical vision of divine creation, the origins of the cosmos, and the hidden spark of light within every human soul. Preserved in four manuscripts discovered at Nag Hammadi and in the Berlin Codex, this gospel offers a breathtaking cosmic drama—one that begins not with sin and shame, but with divine fullness and creative emanation. It is not a narrative of fall, but of forgetting; not a gospel of fear, but of awakening.

At the center of this remarkable text is an intimate and transformative dialogue between the risen Christ and John. Troubled by the suffering and confusion of the world, John retreats into solitude, questioning the meaning of existence. In this moment of despair, Christ appears—not to condemn, but to illuminate. What follows is a spiritual transmission that takes John (and us) beyond time and space, into the very heart of the divine mystery. Jesus does not speak here merely as teacher or savior, but as revealer of the deepest truths—the mysteries that have been hidden from the foundation of the world.

The revelation begins with the One—the ineffable, invisible, and boundless source of all that exists. This divine fullness, or pleroma, is not a person but a pure, formless essence: ungraspable, unnamable, beyond all attributes. From this origin emanates a series of divine beings called aeons—aspects of divine thought, will, and wisdom. Chief among them is Barbelo, the first thought and the mother of all, who participates in the creative process and reflects the fullness of the divine. These aeons do not create in time or space, but through intention and reflection. Their union is pure, harmonious, and sacred—an expression of divine self-knowing and love.

But the story takes a dramatic turn with the emergence of Sophia (Wisdom), an aeon who acts independently in her desire to know the unknowable source. In her yearning, she generates a being without the participation of her divine counterpart. This act disrupts the harmony of the pleroma and results in the birth of a flawed and ignorant entity—Yaldabaoth, also called the Demiurge. Arrogant and unaware of his origin, Yaldabaoth believes himself to be the sole god.

He creates the material world in his image—imperfect, limited, and ruled by ignorance.

This vision is a radical reinterpretation of the Genesis creation story. In the Gnostic telling, the god of the Old Testament is not the true highest God, but a blind and prideful lesser power. The Garden of Eden becomes a site of struggle between imposed ignorance and liberating knowledge. The serpent, often viewed as the deceiver, is reimagined as the bringer of insight. Adam and Eve are not guilty sinners, but divine beings trapped in bodies of flesh, urged toward awakening by the hidden light within them.

Awakening the Divine Spark and the Role of Gnosis

The key to liberation in The Apocryphon of John is gnosis—not knowledge in the conventional sense, but inner revelation, the deep recognition of our divine origin and the awakening of the light within. The human being is portrayed as more than flesh and blood: each person contains a divine spark, a fragment of the true light, hidden beneath layers of forgetfulness and deception. This spark is what makes salvation possible—not through external sacrifice or obedience, but through remembrance.

Christ, in this gospel, is not simply the savior who dies to appease an angry god, but the revealer who comes to open our eyes to what we already are. He is the Light-bearer who descends through the spheres of the lower aeons, bypassing the archons (rulers) who govern the material realm, and enters into the human condition to awaken those ready to receive the truth. His mission is not to create a new religion, but to restore a lost memory: to remind us that we are children of the divine fullness, not slaves to a false creator.

The struggle between light and darkness in this text is not a dualistic standoff between equal powers, but a story of illusion versus reality. The darkness exists only inasmuch as the light is obscured. The archons are powerful only as long as we remain unaware. The material world is not inherently evil, but is a distortion of divine truth—a reflection without substance. When we awaken to the truth within, we are no longer bound by the illusions of the world. We see the false powers for what they are, and we ascend beyond their reach.

This process of awakening is not purely intellectual. It requires spiritual discipline, inner silence, contemplation, and the stripping away of false identities. It involves confronting the fears, desires, and false narratives that bind us. It demands that we stop looking outside ourselves for validation and begin the inner work of listening to the voice of wisdom—the voice that speaks not in thunder, but in stillness. In the Gnostic tradition, this is the path of the initiate, the journey of the soul from exile to homecoming.

The structure of The Apocryphon of John reflects this journey. It moves from cosmic origins to the creation of the world, from the deception of the Demiurge to the implantation of divine spirit in humanity. It offers metaphysical insight, mythological retelling, and practical instruction. It speaks of baptism—not merely as ritual, but as a symbol of purification and rebirth. It describes the ascension of the soul through the celestial realms and the tests it must pass. And it points always to the unshakable truth that we are more than we appear to be.

This modern translation has been prepared with great care to preserve the symbolic richness, philosophical depth, and poetic tone of the original. Every effort has been made to render the text clearly while honoring its sacred mystery. Archaic expressions have been softened, but the spiritual integrity of the message remains untouched. The result is a version that is both readable and reverent—accessible to modern seekers while faithful to its ancient spirit.

To read The Apocryphon of John is to embark on a journey of cosmic remembrance. It is to be challenged, inspired, and awakened. It is to hear the voice of the risen Christ not as a figure of history, but as a living guide who speaks directly to the soul. This is a text that does not ask for passive belief, but for active transformation. It calls you not only to understand, but to become.

Let this book be your companion as you explore the hidden dimensions of existence. Let its words echo in your meditation, its images live in your imagination, and its vision guide you back to the source of your being. In its pages, may you find not only information, but illumination—not only myth, but memory—not only theology, but truth. The truth that you are divine, eternal, and already whole.

Prologue

One day, John, the brother of James (the sons of Zebedee), was walking toward the Temple. A Pharisee named Arimanios approached him and challenged him, asking, "Where is the teacher you used to follow?"

John answered, "He has returned to the place where he came from."

The Pharisee scoffed and said, "That Nazarene deceived you. He filled your minds with lies, hardened your hearts, and led you away from the traditions of your ancestors."

Hearing this, I, John, left the Temple and went to a quiet, deserted mountain. I was troubled and asked myself:

"How was the Savior chosen?
Why did his Father send him into this world?
Who is his Father?
What kind of place will we go to after this life?
He told us, 'This world is just a copy of the eternal one,'
But he never fully explained the eternal world to us."
As I was deep in thought,
Suddenly!

The heavens opened, and a bright light from above
    filled the entire world.
The earth trembled!

I was afraid, but then,
I saw something!
A small child appeared in the light before me.
I watched as he transformed—
First, into an old man,
Then, into a young man again.

I was confused, unable to understand what I was
    seeing.
It was the same person, yet he had different
    appearances within the light.
His image kept shifting, blending into itself.
There were three forms in this vision.

Then he spoke to me:
"John, why do you doubt?
Why are you afraid?
Don't you recognize this image?
There is no reason to fear."

I am always with you.
I am the Father,
The Mother,

The Son.
I am the unbreakable,
The pure.

I have come to teach you
About what is,
What was,
And what will be,
So that you may understand
The unseen world,
The world you can see,
And the eternal, unshaken people of truth.

Lift your head,
Understand my teachings,
And share them with those who have received the
    spirit—
Those who belong to the unshaken people of truth.

The One Beyond Words

The One is above all things. Nothing has power
    over it.
It is the true God,
The Father of everything,
The Holy One,
The invisible ruler of all.

It is untouched,
A pure light too bright for any eye to see.

The One is the Invisible Spirit.
It is beyond what we call "God"—
More than just a god.

Nothing is above it,
Nothing controls it.
Everything exists within it,
Yet it exists within nothing.
It does not depend on anything,
So it is eternal.

It is completely whole and lacks nothing.
It is flawless light.

The One has no limits,
For nothing exists outside it.
The One cannot be examined,
For nothing else exists to compare it to.
The One cannot be measured,
For nothing stands beyond it to measure it.
The One cannot be seen,
For no eyes can perceive it.
The One is forever,
Existing without end.

The One cannot be fully understood,
For no one can grasp its true nature.
The One cannot be described,
For no words are enough.

The One is infinite light,
Pure,
Holy,
Untouched.

The One is beyond understanding,
Forever free from corruption.
Not just "perfect."
Not just "blessed."
Not just "divine."
It is beyond all these things.

It is not physical, yet not without form.
It is not large or small.
It cannot be measured or described
Because it is beyond human understanding.

The One is not just another being among many.
It is far greater—
But even "greater" is not the right word.

It exists beyond space and time.
Anything that exists within space was created.
Anything that exists within time was given time as a
    limit.

The One does not receive anything from anywhere.
It simply knows itself in its own perfect light.

The One is pure majesty.
A majesty that cannot be measured.
It is the source of all realms,
Creating everything that exists.

It is light,
The source of all light.
It is life,
Bringing all life into being.
It is goodness,

From which all goodness flows.
It is knowledge,
The foundation of all wisdom.
It is mercy,
The wellspring of all compassion.
It is generosity,
Giving endlessly without limit.

It does not just have these qualities—
It is the source of them all.

It shines with light beyond measure,
Beyond anything we can understand.

How can I describe it?
Its realm is eternal.
It is a place of peace, silence, and rest,
Existing before everything else.
It is the ruler of all realms,
Sustaining them with its goodness.

The Beginning of All Things

We would know nothing of the indescribable One,
Nothing of the infinite,
If not for the One who came forth from the Father.
Only He has revealed these truths to us.

The Father is surrounded by light.
He sees Himself within this light,
A pure spring of living water
That nourishes all realms.

He sees His reflection in this endless stream of
    Spirit,
Pouring forth from His own being.
He is captivated by the beauty of His own image,
Shining in the light.

From this self-awareness,
His Thought (Ennoia) came into existence.

She appeared before Him,
Shining in the brilliance of His light.
She stood in His presence,
The first power to exist before all things.

She came from the mind of the Father,
The guiding force of all creation.
Her light reflects His light.
She came from His image,
Perfect in strength,
A reflection of the invisible, pure Spirit.

She is the first great power,
The glory of Barbelo,
Radiant among all realms,
Revealing divine majesty.

She gave honor to the Spirit,
Praising Him,
For she came from Him.

She is the first thought,
The image of the Spirit,
The source of all things.

She is:
Mother and Father,
The First Human,
The Holy Spirit,
Threefold Male,
Threefold Power,
Threefold Name,

The eternal and complete realm,
The first to emerge in the unseen world.

Barbelo asked the pure Spirit for foreknowledge,
And the Spirit agreed.
Foreknowledge appeared and stood beside
    Providence.
It came from the Thought of the invisible Spirit.
Foreknowledge praised the Spirit,
And also honored Barbelo,
For she was the reason it came into being.

The Divine Mind Takes Shape

Barbelo asked the Spirit for Incorruptibility,
And the Spirit agreed.
Incorruptibility appeared,
Standing with Thought and Foreknowledge.
It gave honor to the pure Spirit
And to Barbelo,
For she was the reason it came into being.

She asked for Eternal Life,
And the Spirit agreed.
Eternal Life appeared,
Joining the others.
They all gave praise to the invisible Spirit
And to Barbelo,
For she was the reason it came into being.

She asked for Truth,
And the Spirit agreed.
Truth appeared,
Standing with the others.
They all honored the invisible Spirit
And Barbelo,
For she was the reason it came into being.

This is the fivefold realm of the Father:

- The First Human,
- The Image of the Invisible Spirit,
- Providence,
- Barbelo,
- Thought.

Along with:

- Foreknowledge,
- Incorruptibility,
- Everlasting Life,
- Truth.

Since these powers exist in both male and female forms, they create a realm of ten within the Father's domain.

The Expansion of the Divine Mind

The Father looked into Barbelo,
Into the pure light that surrounded the Invisible
    Spirit.
Barbelo conceived and gave birth to a spark of light,
A being full of divine goodness—
Similar to her, but not the same.
This being was her only child,
The only offspring of the Mother-Father,
The only one born from the pure light of the Father.

The Invisible Spirit rejoiced at the light,
Which came forth from the first great power:
Providence,
Barbelo.

The Spirit anointed the child with Goodness,
Making him perfect.
Nothing was lacking in him,
For he was filled with the Goodness of the Invisible
    Spirit.
He stood in the Spirit's presence,
Who poured Goodness upon him.

Having received this blessing,
He immediately gave glory to the Spirit
And to the perfect Providence,
For she was the reason he had come into being.

He then asked for a companion—Mind.
The Spirit agreed,
And when the Invisible Spirit willed it,
Mind came into existence.
Mind stood beside the Anointed One,
Praising the Spirit and Barbelo.
These divine beings were created through silence
    and thought.

He then wished to act through the Word of the
    Invisible Spirit.
The Spirit's Will became Action,
And together with Mind,
It glorified the Light.

Then the Word came into being.
Through this Word,
The divine Son, the Christ,
Created everything.

Everlasting Life, Will,
Mind, and Foreknowledge
All stood together,
Praising the Invisible Spirit and Barbelo,
For she was the reason they had come into existence.

The Completion of the Divine Son

The Holy Spirit helped shape the divine Son,
So that he could stand before the great Invisible
Spirit
As the divine Christ
And glorify Him with a powerful voice.

The Son came through Providence.
The Invisible Spirit gave him authority over
everything.
All rulers and powers were placed beneath him.
The truth within him allowed him to understand all
things.
He was given the highest name of all.

That name will only be revealed to those who are
worthy to hear it.

From the Light, which is Christ,
From the source of purity,
Through a gift of the Spirit,
The Four Lights that came from the divine Son
stood before him.

These Four Lights represent the four great powers:

- Understanding
- Grace
- Perception
- Wisdom

Grace exists in the first Light, called Harmozel, the first angel. With Harmozel are:

- Grace
- Truth
- Form

The second Light is called Oriel, and it rules over the second realm. With Oriel are:

- Insight
- Perception
- Memory

The third Light is called Daveithai, and it rules over the third realm. With Daveithai are:

- Understanding
- Love
- Thought

The fourth Light is called Eleleth, and it rules over the fourth realm. With Eleleth are:

- Perfection
- Peace
- Wisdom

These are the Four Lights that stand before the divine Son.

Twelve realms stand before the Son of Power,
The divine Christ,
Who came into being through the will and grace
Of the Invisible Spirit.

Twelve realms belong to the Son, the divine
    creation.
All of this came into existence
Through the will of the Holy Spirit
And through the power of the divine Son.

From the wisdom of the perfect mind,
Through the will of the Invisible Spirit,
And the desire of the divine Son,
The first perfect human was created.

The Virgin Spirit named this human Adamas
And placed him in the first realm,
With the mighty Christ,

Alongside the first Light, Harmozel,
And its great powers.

The Invisible Spirit gave Adamas a mind of
unshakable strength. Then Adamas spoke, praising the
Invisible Spirit:

"Everything has come from you.
Everything will return to you.
I will praise you and give you glory,
Along with the divine Son,
And the threefold power:
Father, Mother, and Son—
The perfect power of all."
Over the second realm, Adamas's son Seth was
placed,
Along with the second Light, Oriel.

In the third realm, the children of Seth were placed,
Along with the third Light, Daveithai.
(The souls of the saints are there.)

In the fourth realm, the souls of those who were
unaware of the fullness were placed—
Those who did not repent immediately,
But later came to understand and turned back.
They are with the fourth Light, Eleleth.

All of these beings give praise to the Invisible Spirit.

A Crisis That Created the World

At one time, Wisdom (Sophia), a part of the divine
    mind,
Began to think on her own.
She used the power of thought and foreknowledge
That came from the Invisible Spirit.

She wanted to create something from herself,
But she did this without the Spirit's approval
And without the guidance of her masculine
    counterpart,
Who also did not approve.

Without the consent of the Invisible Spirit,
And without her partner's knowledge,
She created something new.

Because she had great power,
Her thought was not empty.
But what she made was imperfect—
Different from herself.

Since she created it alone, without her counterpart,
It was flawed and incomplete,

A being unlike her in form.

When Sophia saw what she had made, she was
     shocked.
It looked like a dragon with a lion's head,
And its eyes flashed like lightning.

She cast it far away from her,
Outside the realm of the immortal beings,
So they would not see it.
(She had created it unknowingly.)

Sophia surrounded it with a bright cloud
And placed a throne in the center of the cloud
So that no one could see it—
Except for the Holy Spirit, known as the Mother of
     the Living.

She named this being Yaldabaoth.

The Rise of Yaldabaoth

Yaldabaoth became the chief ruler.
He took a great amount of power from his mother,
Then left her and moved far from where he was
    created.

He claimed authority for himself,
Building realms of his own,
Using a blazing fire that still burns even now.

The Creation of This World

Yaldabaoth then merged with the chaotic thought
    within himself,
And from this, he began to shape the world.

He created rulers to have authority,
Modeling them after the perfect, unchanging realms
    above.

The first ruler was Athoth.
The second was Harmas, also called the Eye of
    Flame.
The third was Kalilaumbri.
The fourth was Yabel.
The fifth was Adonaiu, also known as Sabaoth.
The sixth was Cain, called the Sun.
The seventh was Abel.
The eighth was Abrisene.
The ninth was Yobel.
The tenth was Armupiel.
The eleventh was Melcheiradonein.
The twelfth was Belias, who rules over the deepest
    part of Hades.

He placed the first seven rulers over the seven levels
of the heavens.
The next five rulers were placed over the deep abyss.

He shared a portion of his fire with them,
But he did not give them any of the Light he had
taken from his mother.

He is a ruler of ignorance and darkness.
When the Light mixed with darkness, the darkness
glowed.
When the darkness mixed with Light, the Light
dimmed.
It was no longer fully Light or fully darkness, but
something in between.
This ruler has three names:

- Yaldabaoth
- Saklas
- Samael

Because he was blinded by his own arrogance, he
made a terrible claim:
"I am God, and there is no other god but me!"
He did not know where his own power had come
from.
His rulers created seven Authorities for themselves,
And each Authority created six demons.

Altogether, there were 365 demons.

These are the names and forms of the seven
    Authorities:

1. Athoth – a sheep's face

2. Eloaios – a donkey's face

3. Astaphaios – a hyena's face

4. Yao – a seven-headed serpent's face

5. Sabaoth – a dragon's face

6. Adonin – a monkey's face

7. Sabbataios – a face of fire and flame

These seven rulers control the days of the week.
Together, they rule over the world.

Yaldabaoth has many faces—
More than all the ones listed.
He can change his form
To appear however he wishes before the seraphim
    who surround him.

Yaldabaoth shared his fire with the seraphim,
But he did not give them any of his pure Light.
Yet, because of the Light he had stolen from his
    mother,
He ruled over them with power and glory.

This is why he called himself God,
Even though he had forgotten where he came from.

He combined the sevenfold Powers of his thoughts
With the Authorities that served him.
He spoke, and it was done.

He gave names to the sevenfold Powers, starting
with the greatest:

- Goodness paired with the first: Athoth
- Providence paired with the second: Eloaios
- Divinity paired with the third: Astaphaios
- Lordship paired with the fourth: Yao
- Kingdom paired with the fifth: Sabaoth
- Zeal paired with the sixth: Adonin
- Understanding paired with the seventh:
  Sabbataios

Each of these rulers had its own realm,
Designed to look like the higher, perfect realms
above.
Each name carried a reflection of the glory of
heaven,
So that one day, Yaldabaoth's demons would be
destroyed.

The demons had names given to them by
    Yaldabaoth,
Names that sounded powerful.
But the names of the Powers, which came from
    above,
Would one day bring down the demons and strip
    them of their power.
That's why each had two names—one of false
    strength and one of true power.

Yaldabaoth copied his creation from a pattern of
    the original, perfect realms above him.
He wanted his world to be like the indestructible
    ones.
But he had never actually seen them.
Instead, the power he had stolen from his mother
Gave him a glimpse of how the higher realms were
    designed.

When he looked at everything he had made,
He turned to the demons that had come from him
    and said,
"I am a jealous God, and there is no other God but
    me!"

But by saying this, he admitted there was another
    God.

For if no other God existed, who would he be
    jealous of?

His mother, Sophia, began to stir restlessly.
She suddenly realized that she had lost the Light
And that her own brightness had dimmed.
Her consort had not approved of what she had done,
So she became even darker.

I asked, "Master, what does it mean that 'she moved
    back and forth'?"
He laughed and said,
"It is not as Moses wrote, 'upon the waters.' Not at
    all."

When Sophia saw what had happened,
When she realized the Light had been stolen by her
    son,
She felt regret.

Lost in ignorance and darkness,
She began to forget who she was.
She felt ashamed.
She wanted to return to the higher realms,
But she could not yet rise back up.

Instead, she wandered restlessly, moving back and
   forth.

Meanwhile, Yaldabaoth, filled with arrogance,
Took even more power from his mother.
Because he was ignorant,
He believed that no one existed except for her.

Yaldabaoth looked at the army of demons he had
   created
And he made himself their ruler, placing himself
   above them.

But when his mother, Sophia, saw what had
   happened,
She realized that her creation was deeply flawed.
She now understood that her consort had never
   approved of what she had done.
Filled with regret, she wept bitterly.

The higher, divine realms heard her cries of
   repentance,
And they asked the Invisible Spirit to help her.
The Spirit agreed
And poured the Holy Spirit over her,
Sending it from the entire divine realm to lift her up.

Translated by Tim Zengerink

Her consort did not come to her directly,
But through the fullness of the divine realm,
Bringing her closer to her original state.

She was raised above her son, Yaldabaoth,
But she was not yet fully restored to where she once
    belonged.
She would have to remain in the ninth realm
Until she could be completely restored.

The Beginning of Humanity

Then a voice rang out from the highest realms,
   declaring:
"The True Human Exists! The Son of Man Exists!"

Yaldabaoth, the ruler of this world, heard the voice
And thought it had come from his mother.
But he did not realize that its true source was:

- The Holy Mother-Father
- The Perfect Providence
- The Image of the Invisible One
- The Father of All, from whom everything was
  created.

The Creation of the First Human

The First Human appeared before them,
Taking the form of a man.

The entire realm of the chief ruler shook!
Even the depths of the abyss trembled!

A great light shined over the waters above the
material world,
And the human's reflection appeared in those
waters.

All the demons and Yaldabaoth, their ruler,
Looked up toward the glowing waters.
Through the light, they saw the Image of the True
Human in the reflection.

The Creation of Adam

Yaldabaoth said to his demons:
"Let us create a man in the image of God and in our
  own likeness,
So that his reflection may give us light."

Each demon used its power to add something to the
  human,
Creating different parts of the man's form,
Based on what they had seen in the divine image
  above them.

They made a physical being
In the likeness of the First Perfect Human
And said,
"We will call him Adam,
For through his name, we will gain the power of
  light."

How They Built the Human Body

The Seven Powers began their work:

- Goodness made the bones
- Providence formed the tendons
- Divinity shaped the flesh
- Lordship created the marrow
- Kingdom made the blood
- Zeal formed the skin
- Understanding created the hair

The army of demons then used these parts to form
    Adam's body,
Putting everything together, piece by piece.
They began with the head:

- Abron made the head
- Meniggesstroeth formed the brain
- Asterechme created the right eye
- Thaspomocha made the left eye
- Ieronumos shaped the right ear
- Bissoum made the left ear
- Akioreim formed the nose
- Banenrphroum created the lips

- Amen shaped the front teeth
- Ibikan formed the molars
- Basiliademe made the tonsils
- Achcha created the uvula

They continued shaping the neck and shoulders:

- Adaban formed the neck
- Chaaman made the neck bones
- Dearcho shaped the throat
- Tebar created the shoulders

Then they worked on the arms and hands:

- Mniarcon made the elbows
- Abitrion shaped the right arm
- Evanthen created the left arm
- Krys made the right hand
- Beluai shaped the left hand
- Treneu formed the fingers of the right hand
- Balbel made the fingers of the left hand
- Kriman created the fingernails

Next, they formed the chest and torso:

- Astrops made the right breast
- Barroph created the left breast
- Baoum shaped the right shoulder joint
- Ararim made the left shoulder joint

- Areche formed the belly
- Phthave created the navel
- Senaphim shaped the abdomen

Then they built the ribs and internal organs:

- Arachethopi made the right ribs
- Zabedo formed the left ribs
- Barias created the right hip
- Phnouth shaped the left hip
- Abenlenarchei made the bone marrow
- Chnoumeninorin shaped the skeleton
- Gesole formed the stomach
- Agromauna made the heart
- Bano created the lungs
- Sostrapal shaped the liver
- Anesimalar made the spleen
- Thopithro formed the intestines
- Biblo created the kidneys

They completed the muscles, veins, and skin:

- Roeror made the sinews
- Taphreo formed the spine
- Ipouspoboba created the veins
- Bineborin made the arteries
- Atoimenpsephei shaped the breath of life

- Entholleia formed the flesh

The lower body was also shaped:

- Bedouk made the right buttock
- Arabeei created the male organ
- Eilo formed the testicles
- Sorma shaped the genitals
- Gormakaiochlabar made the right thigh
- Nebrith shaped the left thigh
- Pserem created the right leg muscles
- Asaklas formed the left leg muscles
- Ormaoth made the right leg
- Emenun shaped the left leg
- Knyx formed the right shin
- Tupelon made the left shin
- Achiel created the right knee
- Phnene shaped the left knee

Finally, they built the feet and toes:

- Phiouthrom made the right foot
- Boabel shaped its toes
- Trachoun created the left foot
- Phikna made its toes
- Miamai formed the toenails

Thus, the demons assembled the human body,
But they had yet to give it life.
The rulers placed in charge of everything were:

- Zathoth

- Armas

- Kalila

- Iabel

- Sabaoth

- Cain

- Abel

The powers that energized different parts of the
body were divided among these beings:

- Diolimodraza controlled the head

- Yammeax controlled the neck

- Yakouib ruled the right shoulder

- Verton ruled the left shoulder

- Oudidi ruled the right hand

- Arbao ruled the left hand

- Lampno ruled the fingers of the right hand

- Leekaphar ruled the fingers of the left hand

- Barbar ruled the right breast

- Imae ruled the left breast

- Pisandriaptes controlled the chest

- Koade controlled the right shoulder joint

- Odeor controlled the left shoulder joint
- Asphixix ruled the right ribs
- Synogchouta ruled the left ribs
- Arouph ruled the abdomen
- Sabalo ruled the womb
- Charcharb ruled the right thigh
- Chthaon ruled the left thigh
- Bathinoth ruled the genitals
- Choux ruled the right leg
- Charcha ruled the left leg
- Aroer ruled the right shin
- Toechtha ruled the left shin
- Aol ruled the right knee
- Charaner ruled the left knee
- Bastan ruled the right foot
- Archentechtha ruled the toes of the right foot
- Marephnounth ruled the left foot
- Abrana ruled the toes of the left foot

The Seven Who Rule the Entire Body:

- Michael
- Ouriel
- Asmenedas
- Saphasatoel
- Aarmouriam

- Richram
- Amiorps

Those in Charge of Human Perception and Thought:

- Archendekta ruled over perception
- Deitharbathas ruled over reception (how things are received)
- Oummaa ruled over imagination
- Aachiaram ruled over reasoning and integration
- Riaramnacho ruled over impulse

The Four Main Forces Behind the Body's Demons:

- Hot – ruled by Phloxopha
- Cold – ruled by Oroorrothos
- Dry – ruled by Erimacho
- Wet – ruled by Athuro

(The mother of all these forces is Onorthochrasaei. She is limitless, blends with all of them, and is the source of matter, which nourishes them.)

The Four Chief Demons That Influence Human Emotions:

- Ephememphi – linked to pleasure
- Yoko – linked to desire
- Nenentophni – linked to distress

- Blaomen – linked to fear

Their mother is EsthesisZouchEpiPtoe, which represents physical sensation.

How Emotions and Passions Arise from These Demons:

Distress leads to:

- Envy
- Jealousy
- Grief
- Anger
- Arguments
- Cruelty
- Worry
- Sorrow

Pleasure leads to:

- Pride (even when undeserved)
- Other harmful desires

Desire leads to:

- Rage
- Fury
- Bitterness
- Frustration
- Dissatisfaction

Fear leads to:

* Terror
* Flattery
* Suffering
* Shame

The ruler of the material soul is Anayo, which belongs to the seven senses (EsthesisZouchEpiPtoe).

In total, there are 365 demons, each playing a role in shaping and completing the psychical and material body.

There were even more beings in charge of different emotions and desires,

but I haven't listed them all here.

If you want to learn more about them,

you can find the details in the Book of Zoroaster.

All of Yaldabaoth's servants and demons

worked together to complete the psychic body of the human.

For a long time, it remained lifeless—

it could not move.

Meanwhile, Yaldabaoth's mother wanted to reclaim the power

she had unknowingly given to the Chief Ruler.

She pleaded with the Most Merciful One,
the MotherFather of everything,
to help her.

Yaldabaoth is Tricked

By divine command, the five Lights were sent down,
disguised as Yaldabaoth's most trusted advisors.
Through their trickery, they caused Yaldabaoth's
    mother's power
to be taken away from him.

They said to Yaldabaoth,
"Breathe your spirit into this man's face,
and he will come to life."

Yaldabaoth did as they said.
He breathed some of his own spirit into the human,
but what he didn't realize was that this spirit
contained his mother's divine power.

Yaldabaoth was completely unaware of what was
    happening— he lived in ignorance.

As soon as his mother's divine power entered the
    human body,
the man came to life!
He grew strong, he shone with light,
and he became filled with knowledge.

The Rulers Become Jealous

Yaldabaoth's demons were jealous of the man.
They had all worked together to form him,
yet now he possessed a power far greater than
    theirs—
greater even than Yaldabaoth's himself.

When they realized that he shined with light,
had more wisdom than they did,
and was free of evil,
they became afraid.

So they took the man
and cast him down
into the lowest, material world,
far from his true home.

The Beginning of Salvation
But the blessed one,
the MotherFather,
the kind and merciful one,
looked down with compassion.

They saw the divine power of the Mother,
which had been stolen and misused by the Chief
    Ruler.
And they prepared a way for salvation to begin.

Since Yaldabaoth's demons might try to overpower
    Adam again,
the Good Spirit sent him a helper out of great
    compassion.

A light-filled Epinoia appeared,
and she was called Life (Zoe).
She worked to restore all creation,
helping Adam and guiding him back to his fullness.

She taught him where his people had come from
and how they could return—
by following the same path they had descended.

The light-filled Epinoia was hidden inside Adam,
so the rulers would not discover her.

She was meant to fix the mistake
that their mother had made.

The Rulers' Plan

Adam was different from his creators—
within him was a shadow of light,
and his mind was greater than theirs.
The rulers and demons looked at him
and saw how powerful his thinking was.

They became jealous and made a plan.
They took fire, earth, water, and wind
and mixed them violently together.
Then they trapped Adam inside a new body made
    of:

* Earth (Matter)
* Water (Darkness)
* Fire (Desire)
* Wind (The False Spirit)

This body became a prison,
a tomb for Adam's spirit.
They chained him to forgetfulness
and made him mortal.

This was the first fall,
the first separation from truth.

But the light-filled Epinoia within him
would awaken his mind and lift him back up.

Adam in Yaldabaoth's Paradise

The rulers placed Adam in their paradise
and told him he could eat freely.

But their food was bitter,
their beauty was corrupt,
their fruit was poison,
and their promises led to death.

They put a tree in the middle of paradise
and called it the Tree of Their Life.
But its life was a lie.

- Its roots were bitter.

- Its branches were dead.

- Its shadow was filled with hatred.

- Its leaves were deception.

- Its flowers held the nectar of wickedness.

- Its fruit brought death.

- Its seeds were full of desire.

- It bloomed in darkness.

Those who ate from it belonged to the underworld,
and darkness became their home.

But there was another tree—
The Tree of the Knowledge of Good and Evil.
This was the Epinoia of Light,
hidden in the garden,
waiting to be discovered.

They forbade Adam from eating from the tree,
standing in front of it to hide it from him.
They were afraid that if he looked up toward the
     fullness of truth,
he would realize his own nakedness and shame.

[But I made them eat from it.
I asked the Savior,
"Lord, wasn't it the serpent who made Adam eat?"
He smiled and said,
"The serpent did this to create a desire for
     reproduction,
so that Adam would become useful to him."]

Yaldabaoth's Trick

Yaldabaoth, the chief ruler, realized that
because of the light-filled Epinoia inside Adam,
his mind was greater than Yaldabaoth's own.
Adam had disobeyed him.

To regain his lost power,
Yaldabaoth made Adam forget everything.

[I asked the Savior, "What does it mean to be
    completely forgetful?"
He answered, "It is not like Moses wrote in his first
    book,
where he said Adam fell into a deep sleep.
Instead, Adam's perception was blocked,
and he became unconscious.
As Yaldabaoth later said through his prophet,
'I will make their minds dull,
so that they do not see or understand.'"]

The Creation of Woman

The light-filled Epinoia hid deep within Adam,
so the Chief Ruler tried to pull her out of him.
But Epinoia could not be captured.
The darkness chased her,
but it couldn't catch her.

Yaldabaoth took some of Adam's power
and used it to create a woman,
shaped to look like the Epinoia he had seen.
He placed the power he took from Adam into her.

[This is not how Moses described it,
when he said, "God took a rib and made the
    woman."]

When Adam saw the woman standing next to him,
the light-filled Epinoia appeared before him.
She removed the veil that had covered his mind.
He woke up from his drunken darkness
and finally recognized his true companion.

He said:
"This is bone from my bones,

and flesh from my flesh."

Because of this, a man will leave his father and
    mother
and be joined to a woman, and the two will become
    one.
They will send a helper to guide him.

[Sophia, our sister, came down,
descending innocently
to reclaim what she had lost.
This is why she was called Life,
the Mother of the Living,
who came from the power of Heaven.
With her help, people can gain perfect knowledge.]

I appeared like an eagle sitting on the Tree of
    Knowledge,
[which is the Epinoia from the pure Light of
    Providence].
I came to teach them
and wake them up from their deep sleep.
[They had fallen, and when they realized they were
    naked,
Epinoia appeared as a being full of light
and opened their minds.]

Yaldabaoth's Curse

When Yaldabaoth saw that they had turned away
    from him,
he cursed the earth.
He found the woman as she was preparing herself
    for her husband.
Because he didn't understand the divine plan,
he made the woman submit to the man as his
    servant.

Adam and Eve were too afraid to reject Yaldabaoth.
But in doing this, he exposed his ignorance to his
    angels.
He threw both of them out of paradise,
covering them in darkness.

Yaldabaoth's Attack on Eve

The Chief Ruler looked at the woman standing with
    Adam.
He saw that she had the light-filled Epinoia inside
    her.
But Yaldabaoth was completely blind to its meaning.

[When Providence saw what was about to happen,
she sent helpers to rescue the Divine Life from Eve.]

But Yaldabaoth attacked Eve.
She gave birth to two sons.

[The first was named Elohim,
the second was named Yahweh.
Elohim had a bear's face,
Yahweh had a cat's face.

One was righteous,
one was not.

Yahweh was righteous,
but Elohim was not.

Yahweh ruled over fire and wind,
while Elohim ruled over water and earth.]

The Beginning of Human Reproduction

Yaldabaoth tricked them, calling them Cain and
    Abel.

[From that moment on, sexual reproduction
    continued,
because the Chief Ruler placed the desire to multiply
    in Eve.
Through intercourse, new human bodies were made,
and Yaldabaoth breathed his artificial spirit into
    them.]

Yaldabaoth gave Cain and Abel control over the
    elements
so they could rule over the material world,
which had become a tomb for the soul.

The Children of Seth Spread
Across the World

Adam joined with the image of his own knowledge
   of the future (foreknowledge).
He had a son, who was like the Son of Man,
And he named him Seth,
Modeling him after the heavenly beings in the
   higher realms.

In the same way, the Mother sent her Spirit,
A reflection of herself,
A model of the perfect divine realm,
To prepare a place for the heavenly beings to
   descend.

But the Chief Ruler made humans drink
From the waters of forgetfulness,
So they wouldn't remember where they truly came
   from.

For a time, the children of Seth lived under this spell.
But when the Spirit comes down from the holy
   realms,

Translated by Tim Zengerink

It will awaken them, heal their weaknesses,
And restore them to the perfect holiness of God.

Six Questions About the Soul

I asked the Savior, "Lord, will every soul be saved
    and enter the pure light?"
He replied, "That is an important question, but it is
    difficult to answer for anyone who is not part of
    the unmoved race.
These are the ones who will receive the Spirit of Life,
And with its power, they will be saved, become
    perfect, and reach greatness.
They remove evil from themselves and care nothing
    for wickedness,
Seeking only what is pure and uncorrupted.

They free themselves from anger, envy, jealousy,
    and selfish desires.
Though they still wear physical bodies, they long for
    the day
When they will be freed from them.
Such people deserve eternal, indestructible life.
They endure hardships with patience,
Knowing that their reward is the gift of everlasting
    life."

I then asked, "Lord, what about those who do not
    do these things, even though the Spirit of Life
    has come to them?"

He answered, "If the Spirit descends upon someone,
    they will be transformed and saved.

Without this Spirit, no one can even stand up.

If, after birth, the Spirit of Life grows in them,

They will gain strength,

And nothing will lead them into wickedness.

But if the artificial spirit takes hold of them,

It will mislead them and lead them away from the
    truth."

I asked, "Lord, when souls leave their bodies, where
    do they go?"

He smiled and said, "If a soul is strong,

It has more of the true power than the artificial spirit,

And so it escapes from evil.

With the help of the Incorruptible One,

That soul is saved and reaches eternal peace."

Then I asked, "Lord, what about those who do not
    know who they truly belong to? Where do their
    souls go?"

He replied, "In these people, the artificial spirit has
    grown too strong,
And they have lost their way.
Their   souls   become   heavy,   drawn   toward
    wickedness,
And they fall into forgetfulness.

When   they   leave   their   bodies,   these   souls   are
    captured by the powers
That the rulers have created.
They are bound in chains and thrown back into the
    cycle again.
They go through this over and over,
Until they free themselves from forgetfulness
By gaining true knowledge.
Only then can they become perfect and be saved."

Finally, I asked, "Lord, how does the soul shrink
    down
So that it can enter a mother's womb or a person?"

He smiled when I asked and said,
"You are truly blessed for understanding this.
The soul must be guided by someone who carries
    the Spirit of Life.
This is how it can be saved and will no longer need
    to enter another body."

Then I asked, "Lord, what happens to the souls of those who once knew the truth but later turned away from it?"

He replied, "They will be taken by demons of emptiness and sent to a place where there is no chance for repentance. They will remain there until the time comes when those who have spoken against the Spirit face their eternal punishment."

I asked, "Lord, where did the artificial spirit come from?"

And he answered:

Three Attempts to Control Humanity

The Holy Mother-Father is kind,
A Spirit full of love and mercy.
Through wisdom and care,
It lifts up the children of the true race,
Helping them grow in understanding and eternal
    light.

But when the Chief Ruler saw humans rising above
    him,
And realized their minds were stronger than his,
He wanted to stop them.
Yet, he did not fully understand their power,
And he failed to block their wisdom.

So he made a plan with his demons,
His loyal followers.
Each of them corrupted Wisdom (Sophia),
And from this came fate—
A final kind of prison.

Fate is unpredictable,
Taking many forms, just like the demons.

It is cruel.
It is stronger than the gods, the rulers, the demons,
And even the generations of people trapped in it.
Fate brought:
Sin, violence, lies, forgetfulness, and confusion,
Heavy rules, crushing guilt,
And deep fear.

Because they were trapped in forgetfulness,
People became blind to the true God.
They could not see their own mistakes.
They were chained to time, seasons,
And ruled by fate.

In time, Yaldabaoth regretted what he had made.
He decided to send a great flood
To wipe out creation and humankind.

But the great light of Providence warned Noah.
Noah spread the message to humanity,
But those who did not know the truth refused to
    listen.

[It did not happen as Moses wrote,
That they hid in an ark.
Instead, they hid in a sacred place,
Not just Noah,

But also many others from the unmoved race.
They hid within a cloud of light.]

Noah understood his own power,
And he knew the divine being that guided him,
Even as the Chief Ruler spread darkness over the
    world.
The Chief Ruler and his demons made a new plan.
They sent demons to the daughters of humans,
Trying to have children with them and take pleasure
    in their company.
But the plan failed.

After that, they tried again.
They created a fake spirit,
A copy of the true Spirit that had come down.

Then, using this false spirit,
The demons tricked women by disguising
    themselves as their husbands.
They filled the women with darkness and evil.

They also created:
Gold and silver,
Money and coins,
Iron and other metals,
And many other material things.

People became obsessed with these things
And were led away from the truth.
They struggled through life,
Grew old without ever feeling true happiness,
And died without ever knowing the real God.

This is how they trapped creation
From the beginning of the world until now.
[They took some women and had children in
    darkness.
They closed their hearts and hardened themselves,
Filling themselves with the false spirit they created,
And this has continued even to this day.]

The Song of Providence

I am the force that guides everything.
I became like my own children.
I have existed since the beginning.
I have walked every path.

I am the treasure of the light.
I am the memory of wholeness.
I stepped into the deepest darkness and kept going.
I entered the very heart of captivity.
The foundations of chaos shook.

I hid because of their evil,
And they did not recognize me.
I came down again,
Determined to complete my mission.

I rose from among those of the light.
I am the reminder of divine care.
I entered the depths of darkness,
Into the center of the underworld,

To fulfill my purpose.
Once again, the foundations of chaos trembled.

The earth shook violently,
Ready to crumble beneath them,
Threatening to destroy everything.

I rose back into the light,
Returning to my place above,
Choosing to wait before bringing judgment.

Then I descended for the third time.
I am the light.
I live in the light.
I carry the memory of divine care.

I entered the deepest darkness,
The very depths of the underworld.
My face shined with light,
For I knew their suffering would soon end.

I stepped into their prison—
For their bodies were like chains holding them
    down.
I called out:
"Wake up!
Rise from your deep sleep!"

The one who had been sleeping awoke,

Tears streaming down,
And cried out:
"Who is calling me?

Where has this hope come from
While I have been trapped here?"

I answered,
"I am the guiding light of divine care.
I am the voice of the Virgin Spirit,
Lifting you to a place of honor.

Stand up!
Remember what you once knew.
Follow the path that leads back to me,
The one who is merciful.

Beware of the demons of poverty.
Beware of the demons of chaos.
Beware of those who seek to keep you trapped.

Wake up!
Stay strong!
Come out of the depths of darkness!"

I lifted him up

And sealed him with the light and water of the five
    seals.
Death could no longer hold him.

Then I returned to the perfect realm,
Completing my purpose.
And now, you have heard it all.

Final Message

"I have told you everything,
So you can write it down
And share it secretly with those who truly belong.
This is the great mystery of those who cannot be
    shaken."

The Savior gave him these words to record and
    protect.
He warned,
"If anyone trades this truth for gifts,
For food,
For drink,
For clothing,
Or for anything else,
They will be cursed."

These words were revealed to John as a mystery.
Then, in an instant, the Savior disappeared.
John went to his fellow disciples
And told them everything the Savior had shared
    with him.
Jesus the Christ.
Amen.

Thank You for Reading

Dear Reader,

We hope this timeless classic has sparked your imagination and enriched your literary journey. Now that you've turned the final page, we want to share a vision for the future of reading—one where every classic you've ever wanted to explore is at your fingertips, in a format that best suits your life.

We'd like to invite you to gain immediate, unlimited digital & audiobook access to hundreds of the most treasured literary classics ever written—along with the option to secure deluxe paperback, hardcover & box set editions at printing cost. Together, we can spark a new global literary renaissance alongside our small, independent publishing house called "The Library of Alexandria."

Thousands of years ago, the Library of Alexandria stood as a beacon of knowledge—until it was lost to history. We aim to reignite that spirit of preservation and discovery right now, in the modern age—only this time, it's accessible to all, in every language and every format.

Picture a world where every timeless classic, novel, poem, or philosophical treatise is not only available to read but also updated for today's readers—modernized, translated into any language or dialect, and ready to enjoy in any format you choose, whether that is in an eBook, audiobook, paperback, or deluxe hardcover & box set version a printing cost.

By joining our movement to rebuild the modern Library of Alexandria, you become part of an unprecedented mission to offer:

- **Unlimited Audiobook & eBook Access to the Greatest Classics of All Time**

   Instantly explore thousands of legendary works, from Plato and Shakespeare to Jane Austen and Leo Tolstoy. All are instantly ready to read or listen to, giving you a complete literary universe at your fingertips.

- **Paperback & Deluxe Editions at Printing Costs:**

   Purchase any title in a paperback, deluxe hardbound, or deluxe boxset edition at printing costs, shipped right to your doorstep. Curate your personal library of Alexandria with editions worthy of display— crafted to last, designed to captivate, and delivered straight to your door.

- **Modern translations for Contemporary Readers in all languages and dialects**

  Discover a vast selection of classics reimagined in clear, current language—no more struggling with outdated phrases or obscure references. Next to the original versions, we aim to offer translations in as many languages and dialects as possible.

  As we continue our translation efforts and add new languages, readers everywhere can connect with these works as if they were written today. By bridging linguistic divides, you're contributing to ensuring that these timeless stories become more meaningful, accessible, and inspiring for people across the globe.

- **Your Personal Library of Alexandria:**

  Over the months and years, you'll curate a unique physical archive of classics—each volume a testament to your taste, curiosity, and love of knowledge. It's not just about owning books—it's about curating a cultural legacy you'll cherish and pass down for generations to come.

- **Join a Global Literary Renaissance:**

  Your support fuels an ongoing mission: allowing us to reinvest in offering deluxe print editions (including special boxsets) at their true cost, broaden the range of available formats and translations, and extend the reach of these works to new audiences worldwide. By joining today, you're not just preserving a legacy of masterpieces; you set in motion a powerful wave of literary accessibility.

We are more than a publisher—we're a movement, and we can't do it alone. Your support lets us scale our mission, preserving and reimagining history's greatest works for tomorrow's readers.

Become a Torchbearer of knowledge.

Thank you for picking up this book and allowing us into your literary journey. As you turn the pages, know that you're part of something larger: a global effort to keep these stories alive, share their wisdom across borders and generations, and spark a true cultural revival for the modern era.

If this resonates with you—please consider taking the next step by visiting:

www.libraryofalexandria.com

With gratitude and a shared love of knowledge,

The Modern Library of Alexandria Team

Visit:

www.libraryofalexandria.com

Or scan the code below:

www.ingramcontent.com/pod-product-compliance
Lightning Source LLC
Chambersburg PA
CBHW011202090426
42742CB00020B/3416